T 18644

4.5

6

MW00700440

DATE DUE

The Potawatomi

by Karen Bush Gibson

Consultants:

Lisa Kraft
Citizen Potawatomi Nation

Donald A. Perrot
Potawatomi Language Instructor
Prairie Band Potawatomi
Hannahville Indian School
Nah Tah Wahsh, PSA

Gary E. Mitchell
Tribal Vice Chairman
Prairie Band Potawatomi Nation

Michael L. Alloway Sr.
Director
Forest County Potawatomi
Cultural Center and Museum

Bridgestone Books
an imprint of Capstone Press
Mankato, Minnesota

Bridgestone Books are published by Capstone Press
151 Good Counsel Drive, P.O. Box 669, Mankato, Minnesota 56002
http://www.capstone-press.com

Library of Congress Cataloging-in-Publication Data
Gibson, Karen Bush.
The Potawatomi/by Karen Bush Gibson.
    p. cm.—(Native peoples)
    Summary: Provides an overview of the past and present lives of the Potawatomi
people, covering their homes, customs and beliefs, government, and more.
    Includes bibliographical references and index.
    ISBN 0-7368-1368-3 (hardcover)
    1. Potawatomi Indians—Juvenile literature. [1. Potawatomi Indians. 2. Indians of North
America.] I. Title. II. Series.
E99.P8 G53 2003
977'.004973—dc21

                            2002000014

Editorial Credits
Rebecca Glaser, editor; Karen Risch, product planning editor; Heidi Meyer, book designer
    and illustrator; Alta Schaffer, photo researcher

Photo Credits
Ann Dallman, 14, 16
Denver Public Library, 10
Irene (Wapskineh) Wheeler (pictured front row, center), Citizen Potawatomi Nation, 6
John A. Barrett Jr., Tribal Chairman, Citizen Potawatomi Nation, 12
John Ellis, 18
Krystal Gouge, cover
Potawatomi Traveling Times, 8, 20

Table of Contents

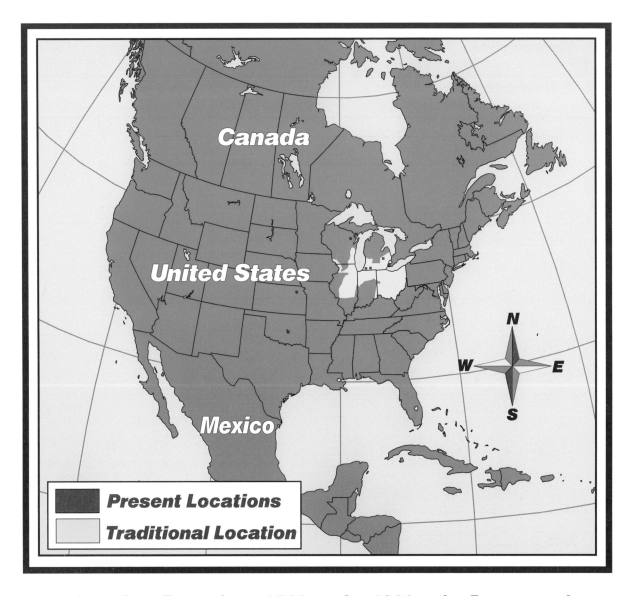

Location: From about 1500 to the 1800s, the Potawatomi lived in the Great Lakes area. Later, the tribe divided into separate nations. Large groups now live in Oklahoma, Kansas, Michigan, Wisconsin, and Canada.

Fast Facts

Today, eight nations of Potawatomi (POT-uh-WOT-uh-mee) live throughout North America. These nations total about 34,000 people. The Potawatomi are also known as "Keepers of the Fire."

Homes: Early Potawatomi lived in bark-covered homes. Summer homes were rectangular. Winter homes were dome shaped. Today, the Potawatomi live in modern houses and apartments.

Food: In the past, the Potawatomi fished and hunted for food. They found food like wild rice, berries, and nuts in nature. The Potawatomi now buy most of their food in grocery stores.

Clothing: Long ago, the Potawatomi wore clothing made from deerskin. They began wearing cloth pants and shirts when they began trading with the French. Potawatomi people now wear modern clothing. They may wear traditional clothing for special events.

Language: The Potawatomi language belongs to the Algonquian language family. Tribes from the northeast coast spoke Algonquian languages.

History

The Potawatomi once lived on the northeast coast of what is now the United States. By 1500, they had moved to the Great Lakes area.

Europeans began coming to the Great Lakes area in the early 1600s. The Potawatomi began trading with the French. By the 1700s, many more people were settling on Potawatomi land.

The U.S. government made more than 40 treaties with the Potawatomi people between 1789 and 1868. The Potawatomi lost more land and rights with each treaty. In 1838, the U.S. government forced the Citizen Potawatomi and the Prairie Band Potawatomi to leave their homes. They traveled from Iowa and Indiana to reservations in Kansas and Oklahoma. As many as 20 people died each day on this journey. The Potawatomi call this journey "The Trail of Death."

Some Potawatomi refused to move to reservations. They moved to Canada or lived with other tribes in Michigan and Wisconsin.

These girls attended St. Mary's Academy, a Catholic boarding school, on the Citizen Potawatomi reservation in Oklahoma. This photo was taken in 1934.

The Potawatomi People

The Potawatomi call themselves Neshnabek. This word means "original people" in their language.

The word Potawatomi comes from the Ojibwa word "Bodewadmi." This word means "people of the place of fire." Bodewadmi was spelled and pronounced many different ways. Potawatomi is the spelling most people use today. Some people still call themselves Neshnabek.

Today, the U.S. government recognizes seven bands of the Potawatomi Nation as independent tribes. Tribal lands are located in Oklahoma, Kansas, Wisconsin, and Michigan. Another Potawatomi nation lives in Canada.

Some Potawatomi live on reservations today. Once there were few jobs on reservations. Conditions of housing, roads, and schools were poor. Reservation life is improving. Tribal businesses and casinos create jobs. Reservation programs provide medical care and schools.

Potawatomi practice many traditional crafts such as basket weaving.

10

Homes, Food, & Clothing

The early Potawatomi built their homes along rivers, streams, and lakes. Summer homes were large rectangular wood lodges, covered with bark or brush. The Potawatomi made winter homes from small trees bent in a dome shape and covered with bark. Today, the Potawatomi live in modern homes.

The Potawatomi once got much of their food from nature. They hunted deer, ducks, and other wild animals. They also fished and farmed. During spring, the Potawatomi tapped maple trees for sap to make syrup. During autumn, the Potawatomi harvested wild rice. Today, Potawatomi families buy their food from grocery stores.

Long ago, Potawatomi men wore deerskin breechcloths, leggings, and fringed shirts. Women wore knee-length dresses decorated with porcupine quills. After trading with the French, some Potawatomi began to wear European clothing. Today, Potawatomi people wear modern clothes.

Potawatomi men began to wear European clothing in the late 1800s after trading with the French.

Potawatomi Government

Before Europeans came to their lands, the Potawatomi did not have a central government. Each village had a council of elders who helped make important decisions. The villages shared clans and a common language. Villages sometimes joined together to fight a common enemy.

Today, most of the nations have a written constitution of laws. People elect their leaders. All Forest County Potawatomi tribal members age 18 and older are part of the General Council. The General Council votes for six people to serve on the Executive Council, which represents all tribal members. One person on the executive council is the tribal chairman.

The Prairie Band Potawatomi of Kansas also votes for a Tribal Council. The seven-member council writes laws for the Prairie Band. The tribal council also helps keep health and education services working for the tribe.

Five justices sit on the Citizen Potawatomi Nation Supreme Court.

The Potawatomi Family

The tribe is like a large family to many Potawatomi people. Grandparents and other elders have a special role in teaching young people about their culture. They often teach children by playing traditional games and telling stories.

The U.S. government sent many Potawatomi children to live at boarding schools during the late 1800s and 1900s. Students lived at these schools far away from their homes. They learned English and Christianity. This religion is based on the teachings of Jesus Christ. Students often waited a long time before they saw their families again.

Today, some Potawatomi children go to tribal reservation schools. They learn about their culture, native language, and other subjects.

Children and adults both study the Potawatomi language.

Potawatomi Religion

Traditionally, religion was a part of Potawatomi daily life. They believed in the Great Spirit and observed him in all of nature.

The Potawatomi practice many ceremonies. Some ceremonies are the naming ceremony, marriage ceremony, and mid-winter ceremony.

Another common ceremony is the smudging ceremony. The Potawatomi hold this ceremony to cleanse their spirits of bad thoughts or sadness. Many Potawatomi participate in this ceremony once a week.

Some Potawatomi belong to the Native American Church. This religion blends native beliefs with Christianity. Four elements make up the Native American Church. They are prayer, singing, use of a plant called peyote, and reflection. This church has more than 250,000 members from many native groups in North America.

Potawatomi people cleanse their spirits during the smudging ceremony.

The Three Fires

Potawatomi elders pass down stories to young people. Elders tell the Potawatomi creation story.

Keshemendo is the Great Spirit. Keshemendo decided the Neshnabek people should move from the northeast coast. The Neshnabek found their new home by following a sacred shell. This Megis shell led them to settle in the Great Lakes area.

Three brothers were the leaders. Each had a special job. The oldest brother, Ojibwa, was named Keeper of the Faith. The middle brother was Ottawa. He was the Keeper of the Trade. Potawatomi was the youngest. He was Keeper of the Sacred Fire. Each leader's group became a separate tribe.

The Potawatomi, Ojibwa, and Ottawa are called the "three fires." All three tribes shared a similar way of life. This story explains how these three tribes came from one single tribe.

Frank Bush of the Pokagon Potawatomi was a well-known storyteller who often told the Three Fires story.

Gatherings

Special gatherings are common among the Potawatomi. Most nations hold events where people to come together and celebrate.

The Citizen Potawatomi hold a Heritage Festival each summer. The Potawatomi play games and talk with old friends. A powwow is a popular part of the Heritage Festival. Tribal members begin dancing during the powwow's Grand Entry. They move in a clockwise direction around the drummers and singers. Some people dress in traditional clothing. Others wear modern clothing. Families honor people with gifts in a tradition called a give-away.

Each summer, the Potawatomi come together for the Gathering of Potawatomi Nations. A different group hosts the gathering each year. A powwow is part of the four-day event. People share their history and culture with one another at this gathering.

Drumming is an important part of Potawatomi powwows.

Hands On: Woodpecker

Many traditional American Indian games were fun and helped children learn skills. Woodpecker is a game that teaches throwing skills. The Potawatomi call pinecones "woodpeckers." Children throw woodpeckers into a small hole in the trunk of a tree. You can make your own woodpecker game.

What You Need

An adult to help
Scissors
Sturdy cardboard box
String or rope

Tape measure
Small piece of rope
Pinecones or small balls
A few players

What You Do

1. Have an adult help cut a hole in the side of the box. The hole should be about 6 inches (15 centimeters) wide.
2. Have the adult hang the box with string or rope from a tree branch or pole about 10 feet (3 meters) above the ground.
3. Measure 10 feet (3 meters) from the cardboard "tree trunk." Place the small rope on the ground to make a line. Players should stand behind this line.
4. Players take turns throwing the pinecones or small balls into the hole. The first player to get six "woodpeckers" inside the cardboard tree trunk wins.

Words to Know

breechcloth (BREECH-kloth)—a piece of deerskin clothing worn hanging from the waist

casino (kuh-SEE-noh)—a place where adults bet money on the outcome of games

clan (KLAN)—a group of related people

cleanse (KLENZ)—to make something clean and pure

constitution (KON-stuh-TOO-shuhn)—an official document that explains the laws of a nation

council (KOUN-suhl)—a group of leaders

powwow (POU-wou)—a social and spiritual celebration of American Indian people that includes dancing

reservation (res-uhr-VAY-shuhn)—land owned and controlled by American Indians

traditional (truh-DISH-uhn-uhl)—using the styles, manners, and ways of the past

treaty (TREE-tee)—an agreement between two nations

Read More

Kubiak, William J. *Great Lakes Indians: A Pictorial Guide.* Grand Rapids, Mich.: Baker Books, 1999.

Maryl, Damon. *The Potawatomi of Wisconsin.* The Library of Native Americans. New York: Rosen Publishing Group's PowerKids Press, 2002.

Powell, Suzanne I. *The Potawatomi.* A First Book. New York: Franklin Watts, 1997.

Useful Addresses and Internet Sites

Citizen Potawatomi Nation
1601 S. Gordon Cooper Drive
Shawnee, OK 74801-8699
http://www.potawatomi.org

Hannahville Indian Community
N14911 Hannahville B-1 Road
Wilson, MI 49896
http://www.hannahville.com

Potawatomi Museum and Cultural Center
5460 Everybody's Road
Crandon, WI 54520
http://www.fcpotawatomi.com/
museum/update.html

Prairie Band Potawatomi Nation
16283 Q Road
Mayetta, KS 66509
http://www.pbpindiantribe.com

Index